Dreamscape with Absinthe

poems by

Elaine Pentaleri

Finishing Line Press
Georgetown, Kentucky

Dreamscape with Absinthe

Copyright © 2026 by Elaine Pentaleri
ISBN 979-8-89990-317-5 First Edition
All rights reserved under International and Pan-American Copyright Conventions. No part of this book may be reproduced in any manner whatsoever without written permission from the publisher, except in the case of brief quotations embodied in critical articles and reviews.

ACKNOWLEDGMENTS

Anderbo.com, "Crepes"
Best of Burlington Writers Workshop, "Yoj"
New Millennium Writings, "Buddhist School of Cosmetology: Lesson One"
Off Channel, "Still Life," "The Last of the Winter Laundry
PhatSalmon, "Metamorphosis of Grief"
Sixty Four Best Poets by the Black Mountain Press, "Clenched Fist," "The Trumpet Player," and "Jolene" (published with a different title)
ZigZagLit, "Apples," "For Charly," and "Bernoulli's Theorem"

Publisher: Leah Huete de Maines
Editor: Christen Kincaid
Cover Art: Susan Smereka
Author Photo: David Savage
Cover Design: Elizabeth Maines McCleavy

Order online: www.finishinglinepress.com
  also available on amazon.com

Author inquiries and mail orders:
Finishing Line Press
PO Box 1626
Georgetown, Kentucky 40324
USA

Contents

Dreamscape with Absinthe 1
Buddhist School of Cosmetology: Lesson One 2
Three Horses 4
Pruning 5
Apples 6
Bartlett Falls 7
Predation 8
Journey of No Return 9
Roses for the Dead 10
A Woman's Gift 11
Yoj 12
Centrifugal Force 13
Enough 14
Treasures 15
Driftwood 16
Dues 17
Slant 18
Tricksters 19
Catching Fire 20
Mrs. Bea 21
Crepes 22
The Other Side 23
Daughter 25
Don't Be Afraid 26
The Trumpet Player 27
Without Gravity 28
Rhinecliff 29
White Balloon 30

Look Out	31
Sibylline	32
Insomnia	33
Interior Decor	34
Jolene	35
Still Life	36
Late	37
Miracle of the Rose	38
Emergence From Negative Space	39
Clenched Fish	40
Square	41
Cake	42
Birthday	43
The Red Dress	44
The Last of the Winter Laundry	45
Song of the Letter K	46
Walk to Her	47
Ascension	48
Bernoulli's Theorem	49
Triptych	50
Metamorphosis of Grief	51
The Tower, 16th Major Arcana of the Tarot	52
Swan Song	53

For Dave, who is by my side in my most far-flung dreams, and—unwaveringly—in real life, too.

Dreamscape with Absinthe

Night tucks in
heavy lidded, close,
draws in, and then
opens luminous green.
The familiar harlequin appears on a zippered stair,
slips through expansive interiors
in forgotten rooms where I have been before and before and before.

I see shadows, only.
This is all I have to go by.
The shadows gesture to me.
This way, this way.

I follow
over to the cliff's edge,
lean and dangle
as far as I can go,
just to see.
It's not that bad.
It's not that far.

The white-runged ladder floats
up into the blueblack sky
and down into the depths of the green.

I know how far I have come
and how far there is to go.

Buddhist School of Cosmetology: Lesson One

A candle
sings inaudibly,
illuminates a small place
against an immeasurable counterpart of unlit space.
A cat in all its soft fur nudges my neck,
unembarrassed at its blatant show of need.
I pet and purr in small places;
this small world I inhabit.
Meanwhile, the stars drone like bees.
At times the trees
that continually redecorate the landscape
are neither beautiful nor ugly.
As I look at them, they disappear.
At times the whorl of space defies mathematics.
The maps of geometry scratch
at immeasurable dimension.
At birth I broke
into a smaller realm,
defined a world through senses,
clutched the air,
grew accustomed to the loud roar of my own breathing.
The small places of candles shed light upon something;
They butt up against the dark.
I empty myself to the questions of prebirth.
Yesterday. There was music from a piano,
flooding space, moving like water.
A thing of this world,
And such a soft perfection of limber hands,
A beauty such as I could hardly bear,
I am turned inside out;
Yesterday was now it isn't anymore.
The dishes are dirty.
I made them that way.
I wash them.
After the ritual with the absinthe,
the bottle is empty.
All continually becomes undone.
After the music, the hands, the undoing, what.
Something I choose to name Beauty, or Power,

extending beyond this circle of light,
beyond geometry
is/or.
From where this pull, this turning inside out,
and what for and why.
I do not want to sleep again.
The night grows larger.
The dishes are clean.
Tomorrow will come,
There will be breakfast, and things to be undone.
On the way to work the mountains and the trees
will spread right there in front of my eyes, beautifully.
I will not hear the drone of stars.

Three Horses

The three horses suddenly
or maybe always are there
beneath the low foliage,
grazing on spring grass,
reincarnated
after the unfortunate incident under the bleachers,
or perhaps the bleachers are an unpleasant mirage
conjured in sleep.
The horses, flicking their long tails
in the languid afternoon heat,
are beautiful
and know the correct responses
to multiple choice questions in arithmetic,
which they deliver in hoofbeats
with astonishing accuracy.
Coming upon them,
their peaceful poetics
and the metaphysics of unstrung theory,
I am compelled to ride one.
I choose the most docile of the three,
grab hold of her abundant mane
and ride off into my past,
back and back into time,
revisiting experience exactly as it once was,
reliving the motives for every act
and thus undoing all regret.
Perhaps this is what dying is.

I wonder if I will ever come back.

Pruning

I am good with plants.
The vegetable garden
interspersed with zinnias
provides through the growing season,
and the perennial beds
run wild with flowers, some unplanned.
My interiors boast a forest of growth.
Even in winter the hoyas
climb, cascade, and drape the living room,
philodendron wind along the ceiling,
ivies trail the brick and twirl around the gurgling fountain.
She gave me a plant before she cut me out:
Rhipsalis Baccifera,
commonly known as the mistletoe cactus.
I have nurtured it for years.
"Be careful," she said.
"If you touch it too much,
the leaves will fall off."
This plant has flourished.
The friendship has not.
I have considered my failures.
Then I considered them again.
Now, decades later, I realize
that this spiky variety,
is perhaps not as lovely as all the others.
I think I will throw it out.

Apples

Getting ready for bed, I hope
for the recurring dream:
    At a bar a woman waits
      in the blackness of her own
        cascading hair, crowned
          with the highlights of her joy.
My days are ruled
as if this were my history.
The apples on the shelf
redden mutely.
Unshined gifts.
The weight of my body surprises me
each time I raise my hand to greet someone.
The abundance of sorrow bends hours.
Tucking itself in, silence
turns easily into
its other.

Bartlett Falls

The woman on the stoney outcrop is reading.
A litter of pine needles flecks the backside of a boulder.

She is reading the paisley pattern
cast by shadows of sunlight
through summer leaves.

Bliss reveals itself through mid-morning.
Granite elephants lounge on the banks, still as stones.

A fortuitous find! A granite desk and chair close up
to the tumbling river and parade of bubbling acrobats.

Surrounding greenery, wise overseers, young mothers
applaud the antics.

Cracks in the ochre rock: a patterned hieroglyphics.
Learn to read! The river roars out the script.
Stones hum in monotones.

The woman is reading the paisley pattern
cast by shadows of sunlight
through summer leaves.

Predation

She was alone in the wild.
Snare. Stone.
Dead rabbit.

The wind blew tangles in her hair.
The river beat inside her
like a pulse.

Stalk. Chase. Ravage.
Ambush. Plunder. Kill.
Hunger. Fervor. Lust.

Restless desire, yearning,
akin to but not
love, precisely.

Journey of No Return

The dark goddess set away
to lands over the sea and far
toward those who linger in the heat,
whose skin like hers was brown,
who knew the changing tides,
of what she left behind and would never see again.

Parting the shadows she made sail for horizons
reached through dream's drawbridge only, through deeper vision
induced by sleep or secret herbs from dark gardens.
Distantly removed from all she once had known,
rich with premonitions and faith in the beyond,
setting sail, there would be no turning back.

The sailors were sea-rocked to a thin nausea,
careening, miles from land. The rhythm of oceans
coursed somewhere beneath the skin, a drumbeat.
Once undertaken the journey was a long one.
There was much at stake.
The full moon fell away to drift and rise again.

The roiling nausea at once was disallowed.
She trembled at betrayal —the uninvited guest— .
History loomed its bold shadows, the unforgotten.
She was struck by the tightness of their grasp on her.
Opening a palm she cradled a small moon in its cup,
released it to its vast and spiraling spin.

Memory and forgetting fell into the sea.
Released from that which came before,
dark goddess touched ground,
made way to the wilder wood.

Roses for the Dead

My father won't come back.
I call to him in the dark.
Those in the shadows plot their betrayals.
In dreams, my mother entreats me.
I walk the night alone.
I want to rise up and dissipate into the air,
scatter myself over rooftops and be released to my death.
Is it possible to present oneself purely?
Truth licks at the borders of deceit.
A black rose garden, the core of a pulpy apple:
when it matters enough I hold open the jaws of the lion,
become the jaws of the lion, and roar.
The lake lashes at the icy air.
The thin arms of winter trees bend delicately,
straining toward cataclysm.
The sandy beach remains soft, remembering summer:
tufted lake grasses, quilted beach blankets,
hot afternoon sun.
Something small and warm bursts inside me,
rose cocoon, small birth.
I am strengthened by this passage through hell.
I switch the December horse into this dark night.
The hands on the clock are clapping.
I'm off.

A Woman's Gift

Mind shattering
in the thick/ black night;
between sleeping and waking
patterns crack like lightning in
the mind's wide sky.
      Recreation,
      Divination,
      Vision.
Shifts in the reeling heat of dreams'
undulations, swirling in
blue imaginings
lifting to wider
          space
          distance
              stillness
She sees it.
A new way.

Yoj

I cannot talk about god anymore.
The waitress is here again with another brandy.
I swill my drink and gaze off absently.
You ask if i'd mind
if you went alone to see the movie about
the woman who swills her drink and gazes off absently.
I cannot throw out old letters.
I cannot avoid ardent infatuation.
I cannot stay put.
The palm islands are far away
and dotted with hotels and
limos lace the airports and
there are discos everywhere.
No one wants to talk about the psychedelic renaissance anymore.
I can not write with my left hand.
I note the incipience of traffic jams
in the queen city at 7:30 in the morning.
I cannot whistle or stand on my head.
I cannot stay out of cafes or do a back dive
or have a headache instead of sex.
I cannot be happy at weddings
or read War and Peace
or drink scotch straight or erase 3 o'clock.
and when I spell out joy backwards
it says (I think) Yoj.
And that can mean anything
that you want.

Centrifugal Force

It was summer and the afternoons were charged
with lightning and thunder
Dramatic prologue.
Grand *a priori*.
Such theater.
Late nights after the rains
city streets revealed a puddled moon,
like language, mistaken for what it seemed.
Beyond seeming, above, a solar eclipse
in space and time, the interstice— .
Stars free float
spinning in the wide indigo.

The small words of image moons
faintly echo the songs of ruling stars
singing:
faith is not stuff   but   air—.
Released to a darkening spin
we are what lies between.

Enough

The farm will be left behind.
Plowed earth. Potatoes. Tied burlap.
The woman with her baby
inside will be fine enough.
The farm is far from the landing strip
and the landing strip runs parallel to the expressway
which is a four lane gridlock.
The cows have grown accustomed
to the roar of aircraft.
There is food in the pantry,
silage has been put up for winter,
and the river drains lazily along the cow field,
past yellow wood sorrel and purple cornflower,
down into the hollow
in its ardent search for return
to mangroves, salt marshes, seagrasses,
and the wide belly of the sea.
The aircraft overhead lifts away to amenities.
The condos at Seabreeze
rest in tight neat rows on the blacktop
and reach for a view.
Everything is clean,
with good coffee,
whatever you want.
The ocean will swallow it all whole in one gulp,
take it back into the wide sea belly.
The newspaper warns:
Tidal flooding, sea level rise, and heavy precipitation events
Threaten the trillion-dollar coastal property market.
Hydrodynamic surge models predict
increased hurricane flood risk at the coast.
A storm surge, a wall of water,
will tumble it all in widespread devastation.
The farm will be left behind.
Plowed earth. Potatoes. Tied burlap.
The woman and her baby
will be fine enough.

Treasures

She shipped small treasures.
That's like putting five hundred bucks
right in your pocket
in a trinket shop in Damascus
and when you reach in to grab some
small birds by the hundreds
take to the sky.

Driftwood

There are shells strung from a piece of driftwood
out on the back porch.
The language of wind chimes is as evasive as its player.
I'll stay, he said.

Melodious laughter rises
on the swells of the breeze,
trilling up into the rustling leaves.

Goodbye, sweet dreamer.

Dues

A fistful of coins from under the couch cushions
is tossed into the sky:
Toll.
Easy Pass. At last,
access through the pearly gates.
Glinting silver pieces scatter
up into an opaque wonderland infused with light;
I follow.

Think of a kite snapping:
A world of reeling images,
what flashes before your eyes,
a dreamscape.

Ascension into clouds:
soft, light,
an easy, flirting lift.

The earthly performers
are weighted down to the theater stage,
the sooty floor staining their bare feet.
This script demands a careful pace.
The third act is especially clever
and poignant and
on opening day
the audience laughs
and weeps.

Slant

Are we alone?
the autumn light, a bowl of apples,
strangers in their own land.
Variations seem easy to explain:
the tavern will feature jesters and lively tunes.
A window frame splits the view:
colorful scarves, embroidered caps,
painted ceilings,
the promise of expanding.
everyone carries something.

Tricksters

The rain did come,
beginning gently then
slicing through the purple afternoon.
A pattern etched in a wheatfield
had once again
confounded the villagers.
The pranksters drop by for lunch,
set off into the woods
tumbling as they go
off into the leafy green,
so far gone from view
I'll have to dream them back.

Catching Fire

I can save up to three lives.
What inspired this?
A pad scribbled with lunch dates,
yellow discount tags,
an Italian magazine.
I am likely to say things ordinarily kept secret,
to separate myself from others, and from what I did before,
soften the awkwardness with crates of roses,
a dark exotic centerpiece,
turn attentions to the constellations.
A discerning audience
might notice the provocative sculptures
the mainstream media had ignored.
> Jung's red book of crystal visions revived,
> a fantastical interior decor
> unfurling like the green of a new leaf,
> catching fire.

Turn
toward mysterious disappearances.
Don't forget.

Mrs. Bea

Time is a playground.
This is about sliding forward or back,
and tetherball.

I have been thinking about this again, yesterday,
and again the day after tomorrow,
because Nancy died.

This is about jumping rope,
and perhaps there is more to that:
those playing double-dutch learn right away
to honor the rhythm and the rope's sway,
—listen: it's a metronome—
how they jump out and back in
taking turns that way.
Or swinging,
with hands reaching deftly to the next bar.
Joy undulates along the sound waves of distant shouts
from the children on the pitch playing ball tag.
Chin up!
Peer over the parallel bar.
See?
Robbie and Rosie at four square,
and Mrs. Bea on her whistle:
"Everyone in!"
This is about sliding
up and down and for or aft,
about going out and coming back,
tearing at the fabric,
unzipping the line of stars,
stepping up and over this reality, out,
      (just to see, just to try it, visit the playground in the other
      neighborhood)
and then, stepping back in again,
to find everything the same
exactly as it was, when.

Crepes

4:13
Purposely
I sit where you might find me
and where you might not.
The fountain spouts water.
You never noticed how the sun
catches the crest of spray.
There wasn't enough time
and you were occupied with other things.
4:19
On the digital watchface.
I wait for a chance encounter,
to show you the spray of water,
and how the sun catches its crest.
I want nothing but that.
4:22
I think you won't come.
I like the way you sway your arms when you dance.
4:25
I wonder what you might regret,
and how I could leave you happy.
4:29
I go quickly. There isn't much time.
4:30
You walk by.
I asked you once if you were happy. No.
Alone, I go
out to a clean, well-lit place. Praline crepes.
My tarot cards are blank.
I do not wish I was someplace else.

The Other Side

the ambiguity curve. fire. predictable. of
    god. a jaunt to utah, affectionately suggested.
if you would stay all night.
      the white stone houses lend clarity
        to the muted grey/green sky.
    gusts of a sticky summer,
        the flames of four candles.
    if I could let this go—
I was not at home.
I could create this darkness.
what i was looking for—
    the poem. the other side. hands.
      I hope I never do.
        who has time, for god's sake.
          my initiative.
            laden with light. turbulent. persistent. I don't
expect much.
she didn't confirm or deny anything.
    disappearing, all she wanted.
      a theatrical gesture. a kind of love. there are
        some differences. experiences. sunday morning,
      that she was a lesbian.
    what can be described by us upon a moment.
      the wind's cadence. other people's love.
        ebony pages of history. her muscular form.
          cliffstones. that I should run into.
        I had to drive down. I won't go that far.
      she wants to continue.
I could live on that.
her lunch break.
we would want to change things.
I am going with this life.
                      maybe we can meet
somewhere.
    the nature of power/
      the last cherished starling.
        empty places, once begun, cling
          relentlessly.
          earlier in the afternoon her forehead

/the lake between mountains/
  inclined to listen, a meaningful endeavor,
I drink myself into oblivion.
if perhaps we became sexual,
          what we have rehearsed, slate gray, like this pencil.
     a diagonal crossing. a heady psychedelic groove.
   a portrait i cannot change.
  as long as there's a reason.
I adore you.
I am drunker than I think.

Daughter

Untouched for years:
the marble's irregular mass,
at certain angles mottled in its effect,
sure as stone.
Over time
clouds scud across the overarching sky,
aching in the hollows of translucent blue,
sucking at my life.
When I am far enough in
and delirious from the altitude and
lack of air
she slices through the cool stone
to its reveal.
The sky is now a brilliant blue
with low, fat clouds
moving so quickly my mind reels.
Such beauty!
I had only dared to presume.
Its expansiveness takes my breath away.
Poised for detail
she carves into the stone's eye
an exalted glance.
Stone smoothed to its best advantage,
a casual looking back.
She puts away her carving tools.
For what I have known to be true,
my heart aches.

Don't Be Afraid

The chair once held you. Pretend that everything is as it was.
I'll be the baby. No, I'll be the father,
and I am coming home from work. You can be the Scout.
You can rub two sticks together and watch them ignite.

The pile of snow at the head of the drive
is heavy and quiet, not like the car alarm.
The off switch.
Prerogatives.

The cat is still on the porch despite the noise from the chainsaw.
At the mirror, a nick from shaving.
In the woods, stuffed animals, stuffed chairs,
and a forest of sticky notes.

Things to do.
 A list:
 Confirm friendship. Go to the party.
Call the daughter. Someone needs to phone the daughter.
The daughter is made of wax.
The daughter is waiting for a call.
The daughter might come back in another form,
perhaps a book jacket or a marble sphinx
or the Northern Lights. It's hard to say.
Create order from chaos. Construct illusions by folding
laundry into neat piles, the sleeves tucked under.
Then, toss it into the back of the car. Turn on the ignition.

Drive.

The Trumpet Player

A skeletal outline, a figure, a face
a particular response s/he makes
me hungry. I swallow the sea,
fall back on, turning under, a wave
returning. There is a quiet place, fathoms I forgot
my car keys.
The engine won't turn
over. Far below a woman
sings the water drives
her gurgling song under
what one can imagine only.
An amber light, tangent ray
spreads itself at first unnoticed down
into the depths of the green.
S/he brings me
to.
I drive for hours, am always there.
We fall   under   this way
into.

Without Gravity

Picture the clinking of glasses, white napkins,
pretty people at the reception
toasting their accomplishments.
I can be a diaphanous sylph
and hover near the crystal chandelier.

Cheers!

The question is how to rise.
Bundled in dream, anything is possible.
Like when the cyclist
approaching at top speed in my lane
crashes into me,
and we slide into one another,
share body space
mingle for a moment,
truly collide.
The question is how do we live our lives.

When we clink our glasses they shatter
into a million pieces
and take to the sky.

Rhinecliff

I spill and flood myself into the moment,
surging out of darkness into darkness
waves of light and despair,
grief, power, love,
the gathering mountains,
the circling gulls,
outside and inside myself.
Water, crystal ice
reflects the grief/joy
that pours from my skin,
enshrouding the surrounding air-.
Pain/ pleasure intermingle,
my heart, body and mind
are driven
to an edge and compelled to fall,
to be carried and to carry it all.
I cry, die, fly, fall,
taken by the moment, the time,
knowing only that it is
mine.

White Balloon

Unknown, familiar thing,
white balloon,
lifted from the leaden clouds.
Primeval wolves sing.
A luminous pull draws the earth
back from the deep,
unstopping the stone
from the cavernous soul,
until a flood of yearnings is unleashed.
From the bountiful Sea:
ardent, illuminant,
insatiate that only Death
might appease.
Unknown, familiar thing,
/my love/
tonight, turbulent and dark,
sky and sea/
Sing.

Look Out

Curling in
      to a book,
      the screen's vortex,
      myself,
      interiors.
Enough.

I gasp for air,
seek breath and vantage,
pull to a stand,
walk out and over
to the blue edge,
look out.

See what the lake will wash over and embrace,
what the mountain will enshroud,
what drifts skyward
softened by clouds,
how the internal noise quiets.

See the mountains,
look—
they circle the silver lake,
mound one upon the other
like thick blue hearts
giving off their steamy heat.

Sibylline

In the lilt and drift of girlhood,
buoyed by tinny piano notes,
I fell from the window ledge
and took to flying.
This went on for some heedless time.

I stuck the landing on stone ground,
and despite some toughened skin around a scar
I was essentially unharmed,
if not shaken from reverie.

I quickly understood the rules of the game,
which I played especially well:
how to bounce back into the air
after hitting a hard surface,
how to reascend.

Insomnia

Thought/ kite

b   bb
    o   in   g

in the afternoon.
Rag-tailed quadrangle,
unfettered to a free float.
Little reveries:
freedom of movement,
improvisation,
poem!

Later at dream's drawbridge
the night sky swirls
its blue-black density.
Windfall gust
catches the kite /just/
in the snag
and won't be unloosed.
Sinister branch.
Claw.
Screech owl.
Dark reduction.

Nefarious muse.

Interior Décor

On her side
nude on the velvet couch
she dreamed the recurring dream,
spiraling toward a distant point,
(the apex of the mind's interior).
 He watched her from the armchair.

Later,
she googled upholstery fabric
and was convinced again
she had the right kind,
and bought a dress with the same velvet design.
She never wore it,
liking instead the way it hung
in the closet.

Each morning he would go to the dress
and carry it out on its hanger.
"Wear this."

Outside the birches
lift their arms jubilant and wide
cradling the scope of the sky,
and she imagines herself flying.

Jolene

I went to her house to watch home videos and
they made love beside me on the bed and
I fell into the eye of a cat that toyed and played
with the saxophone dangling from a black ribbon
on the brass.

Sometimes I write about people I actually know.

I like an apartment sparse/
especially under the bed.

Moving in with her I
cleared the counter of the flowers and lace
and gloves, revealing a clean wood surface
the starkness of which compelled her to
put me out.

Back home I scrubbed the white porcelain sink,
which pleased me.
Far from/   fire form/   worn warm world
the word hurled. Her.

When lights dim it is as if suddenly the dinner hour is over.
I stared absently at my thumbnail. Going back
to New York the red polish left smears across the walls.
I like them white.

Around his neck a thin black tie a
sexual power a brass longing, something
that was a promise resembling but not quite an
immediate death.

Still Life

Fidelity has nothing to do (with anything).
Any act is worth more
than any denial.

Fear nothing.
Distance becomes me.
I will continually unlock your lie,
open it up to space.
Everything is at stake
(all
ways).
The painting has a certain almost warm effect
when it hangs within the details of my house.
From a twenty-yard perspective
(perhaps out on the neighbor's lawn)
(or the view from the window)
the painting (still) is.

I would not want you to write
the same poem again.

I love the haloed you-ness,
its promise never
to remain the same.
Go with me from me. Go-
I love/you are.

Late

From a thorn in my side
a red rose blooms full.
Immaculate Misconception.

Miracle of the Rose
For Jean Genet

Her winged woman's body
is poised in the streetlamp light.
She is unafraid.
Thieves scramble,
fractured in the low light,
tumbling off the hoods of automobiles
into the madcap night,
derelict with possibility, sound, timbre.
Holiness dances with turpitude,
illusory, and the same.
Messages drift through
a steamy circuitous past:
All we ever knew or will know
is the same as it ever was.

Which allies are most likely to help you?
Would you look for them?
Would you see them in the thick night air?
She unleashes the starkness of her fertility,
stands there,
dense with dirt.

Emergence From Negative Space

```
          Draw open the heavy velvet    /what we move through/
              Push!/:The top hat           the white tipped wand, the gloves
                    hover                  in midair.
                       Such                   tricks!
                  The rabbit is                pulled by its ears
           and set scampering                  down the rabbit hole.
       The dove is released                 to the sky.
       All the dreams we                       follow out or over
              are elusive                   and wild
       /the weight of                          uncertainty/
              /so much                         depends upon/.

          And what of                         the final act,
             (not the trick              to disappear; the other; this is the other)
              revealed in                    the parting mist.
       After all the                       conjuring,
        the secret                             language
       and faith                            in thin air,
       a believing eye                        might begin to discern
        the thin                            diaphanous film
       A hint of blue      in the cloak     perhaps.
       She has             been             practicing   for years.
           Can             you  see         her?
       Can                 you              see?
```

Clenched Fish

The apartment is overstuffed with books and coffee.
Sometimes a fish swims by the window and peers in,
Its broad eye unblinking,
As full and unfull of judgment
As the eye of god unlooking.
Everything is fine spun wool.
The cricket's scissor call is far away
But I can hear the forecasted weather.
Now and now it is not winter,
Not the whorl of snow/ the crystal ice world
That cracks open like a dream on the edge of waking.
I am so close to everything I cannot see.
Sometimes without (him) I think I do not remember.
The other. What it would be like.
I face away from him toward the candle,
Whisper random speculations/ what else/ might be
I sing to the candle flame/ I hear his breathing.
In this I do not know the other,
Nor what chains I solder.
I have heard from gods and crickets
that snow will come unfleecing.
I hold tight to nothing like a glove.

Square

The room was square and full of an abundance of nothing
and light which fell spaciously across gleaming floors.
The window was open.
The breeze rustled nothing,
exquisitely,
for lack of curtains.
The intangibility of the possible was everywhere.

cake

you
sport a hat talk of foreign places and passports the familiar half
—drunk quart of beer in the fridge an old dog longing to be trans-
formed perhaps in london or cannes on a hillside strewn with
roses women at the border a deer in the backseat of a car two
turkey hearts you forgot to buy dish soap i would say a vodka
with olives or a book by kerouac

move
shadows a comfortable shroud an obscure lack of expectancy
a mingling place for two diverse solitudes foreign magic an
alchemist of dreams a poem a guru a drunken old man calls
the cops somewhere in a funky hotel in the latin quarter of
paris walking up a hill laden with cherry trees and young girls

me
toward floods of thought a biograph a particular silence
what i have gained by your presence a red armchair a bit of
LSD the way you swing your arms when you dance some kind
of destiny true to a name a primitive unraveling someone
whom i deeply love its february again and someone spilled
eggs and cream all over the cake again a year ago i never
would have guessed how much.

birthday

when I wrap myself up
in insignificance
I never forget the ribbon,
just in case.

The Red Dress

Isadora,
I write to you again. I am wearing the red dress. How
right that we have never met. Then, I can tell you everything,
and trust you to hear the details of this odd
progression, the odd words which in the face of change
find expression. You danced your patterns out,
barefoot in the grass, beautiful in the heedlessness
of your way, true to no truth but your own, valuing
alone the force that drove you. I have loved hard, been
full, loved you. I have become the dance, the dress, the
change, loved all that is beautiful and strange, and am
forever delivered, new. I have kept my butterflies in an
open hand. They are beautiful, and more so, somehow,
when they go.

The Last of the Winter Laundry

Down/the street
carrying (the sun's out)
the weight of the world.
Project #1: to move the earth.
(toward.)
(Leverage. The axis.)
A box of Cheer,
an agitator,
suds,
some talk of rolled trousers,
thin tee shirts,
porch barbeques.
Behind the glass of the washer
the faces that color my world
seem to appear,
churning in the soap bubbles.
The Cornucopia.
(This, after everything: dank
February, trying not to bore myself,
the apology, what I said-)
Now on the brink of.
Harbinger.
Rites of.

Song of the Letter K

The sound is mine. I own it. Assertive, distinct.
Look at me:
Strong backbone, solid stance,
A welcoming gesture, reaching out.
          K.
A true original.
I am not afraid to stand alone,
informal but clear in my affirmations,
as in the short and sweet text message:
"K!"
I do not even need to depend on a vowel.
I've got this.
Folks might not recognize my contributions.
I am a middle child, lost between A and Z.
C is sure to arrive first
with her curves and soft hair.
Notice how C cuts
into my spaces. It's a constant reckoning.
Cat should be mine, as well as crisp, and clean,
clarity, conscience, cooperation.
C can not build *character* on her own,
leaning on h for support,
does not know her own mind.
A copycat, C plagiarizes the work of sister S,
who has curves of her own and really is not to be messed with.
Look how C sneaks in on scissor and sciences,
jumps in ahead on stack and brick, sock and clock,
fiddlestick, diamondback, lock,
Stealing the thunder, taking credit.
Well, I offer you kite, kayak, kiss, and kindness,
karma, kitten, kibbutz, and keep.
That is what is left in the wake.

Walk to Her

I left the bicycle parked in the silver rain/
splattered chain/ cast iron/ a balustrade;
walked to her
> past the colors of poverty's flat urban edge:
> the lavender grown leggy
> from lack of water,
> the Tibetan prayer flags yellow and crimson,
> sidewalk streets lined with broken
> furniture/ appliances/ small swaths
> of untended lawn/ children
> peering out of screen doors
> hungry for out.
> doors open
> intermittently and slam again
> for want of a porch.
> the brindle boxer on the upstairs balcony,
> paws poised on the rail,
> is ready to make a go for it,
> he's thinkin' of jumpin',
> he's considering the distance,
> maybe twelve feet,
> it might be worth it.

house; she wasn't there,
wasn't in
the austerity of the tall chairs, the Turkish rug.
she slid the extension ladder closed
and secured it to the truck bed.
By then the rain had stopped. The rain
was an intermittent drizzle on her windshield.
By the time I got back to the bicycle it wasn't
even wet and the sun blazed over the lake.
I am not sure if she was home or not.
I think I walked.
If I ride
all the way to the chevrolet dealership
I will never get out alive.

Ascension
    For Agnes Martin

Floating, arms stretched, above
the   -horizontal-
in/to the amorphous rose   washed light
or gradually rising from a chair,
the canvas of mind spread
open   /and   laughter
emptying in.

But today
a bicycle wheel strains
heavy against   /cracks/
in the asphalt gray,
presses the
vertical
pushing
up   in/ to   the darkening mercurial sky/ and
it begins to rain.

Bernoulli's Theorem

Throw caution to the wind.
Icarus,
I sent the kite up first, for a test run.
The kite
slowed
and fell toward the earth
dragging
its golden key,
bumping repeatedly
along the grass
until kite and tail
came to rest
in a gentle field.
I jumped for the free fall anyway.
Unlocked the sky.
Generated lift to oppose the weight.
Dangled the kite by the string from my hand,
let the line
slip through my fingers, and
Letting the wind catch it,
flew.

Triptych

The house rests sturdy beneath
tree limbs that lean up against
hills that roll up close to
the mountainsides mounding green
upon lumps of cloud.
You can poke a finger through
And watch until the translucent blue runs out all over.
That is why the sky goes on forever like that.

I posted something today on god's wall.
Picked up some spray paint,
Day Glo Pink from the local hardware,
and had a go at The Gate.
Such graffiti art is gratifying.
What I got was Time. More of it.
A promissory note.
God is not ready for me, yet.
Certainly
I am not ready for god.

The aesthetics of this day might cause me
to sing something especially beautiful,
or dance.
The raucous crow
outside the window,
knows everything I know
and more besides,
and like me
strengthens her raven wings
by virtue of the thrust of wind,
never wishing for a quiet life.

Metamorphosis of Grief

Nothing, like this.
Something glints on the creek bottom,
A golden leaf dropped last autumn.
The resilience of spring will not hold
The tension between your hand and the wire,
Or suspend an iron pot over the cook fire,
Or whittle beyond the green
To the heart's white center.
The fire ignites without you.
Boughs, limbs, trunks of trees
Stacked eight feet high
Burst into raging flames
Roaring your name into the hungry dark,
Burning all night, yet small against immensity.
The dark swallows you whole,
Pulls you farther and farther back
Like this.

The Tower, 16th Major Arcana of the Tarot

The struggling elegance of this storm.
Tower of chaos, disordered spirits,
smoky torpor,
a thrashing falling firestorm star.

This upheaval is one among hundreds,
but consider the possibilities.
Coins, brash chess queens, babies,
a black cowboy hat, tumbling.

What accident will swell, rupture, and overturn,
surprising us with its strangeness?
This is salvation by fire and water.
A beauty.

Swan Song

Between splatters of rain and swaths of solitude
The Jerusalem Trail winds up a Vermont mountainside   thick and overgrown.
Thoughts are let loose like birds singing.
The summit is glorious:
                    a crossroad.
"Your poems end well," she said.
Which is perhaps the point.
To arrange the final act
The farewell party
I would prefer a little time   but not too much to say
good   the joy of you has moved me
bye   through the overgrowth, and has sung to me like birds
as if I could ever say enough.
In Vermont one can be buried on one's own land
without mandate for
caskets
embalming serums
stuffy parlors
showings.
       <u>Recipe</u>
(Must be made with me at home)
Ingredients:
Beds, down quilts, shawls, in a variety of colors, strewn about, many, for guests,
arrays of friends and family, mixed, sweetened by time and trouble, all.
       (The most surprising guests of all will come.)
Poems, many.
Singing, much.
Soup, in abundance.
Crusty bread, same.
Honey, organic, raw, jars of it.
Tea, bountiful.
Libations, cascading.
Wood-fires, continually.
Flowers, wild or from the garden, many.
A wooden box, one.
       Reserve the flowers and box until needed.
Mix all ingredients liberally, in my house, the one that Dave built for us.

Simmer on low heat for several days until softened.
As sadness and forgiveness melt
           insensitivities
                      failures
                                    apologies.
Story and laughter will bubble up.
Take turns stirring gently until again well mixed.
There will be Raia's clever remembrances.
Tess will play and sing the song she wrote for me,
the funny and poignant one
and everyone will laugh.
        Rain will come.
        Open the windows.
        Throw flowers to sweeten the passage.

Thank you for coming.

Elaine Pentaleri lives in rural Vermont on 22 acres of field, woodland, and stream. A feminist, spiritualist, outdoor enthusiast, and active reader and writer of poetry, Pentaleri has a particular interest in cultivating dynamic literary communities and bringing publishing opportunities to life.

Pentaleri served as board co-chair of The Burlington Writers Workshop from 2018 – 2021, where she managed the various aspects of the organization and worked to provide writers with free learning opportunities that help them develop as writers. As co-chair of Burlington Writers Workshop, Pentaleri edited the international online literary publication *Mud Season Review* in 2020 and 2021 and she revitalized the Burlington Writers Workshops' annual print edition of *Cold Lake Anthology* from 2018 – 2022. Pentaleri is the founder of The Green Mountain Book. Festival, inaugurated in 2022, an annual celebration of the literary arts in Burlington, Vermont. Pentaleri's poetry has appeared in various small press and online publications.

www.ingramcontent.com/pod-product-compliance
Lightning Source LLC
Chambersburg PA
CBHW030059170426
43197CB00010B/1587